Dropping In On...

KENYA

David C. King

A Geography Series

ROURKE BOOK COMPANY, INC.
VERO BEACH, FLORIDA 32964

Printed in the United States of America

Revised Edition 2004

Library of Congress Cataloging-in-Publication Data

King, David C.
    Kenya / by David C. King.
        p.   cm. — (Dropping in on)
    Includes index.
    ISBN 1-55916-083-7
    1. Kenya—Juvenile literature. I. Title.
II. Series.
    DT433.522.K56   1995
    967.62—dc20   95-10079
                                                    CIP
                                                    AC

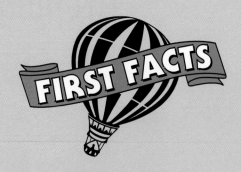

Kenya
■ ■ ■ ■ ■ ■ ■ ■ ■

Official Name: Republic of Kenya

Area: 224,960 square miles

Population: 31,139,00

Capital: Nairobi

Largest City: Nairobi (pop. 2,343,000)

Highest Elevation:
Mt. Kenya (17,058 feet)

Official Languages: Swahili and English

Major Religions: Protestant, Roman Catholic, and Muslim

Money: Shilling

Form of Government: Republic

Flag:

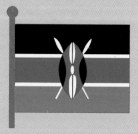

TABLE OF CONTENTS

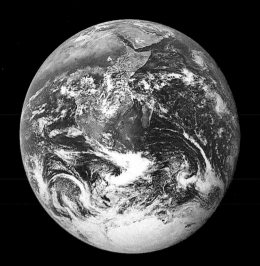

Our Blue Ball—The Earth

The Earth can be divided into two hemispheres. The word hemisphere means "half a ball"—in this case, the ball is the Earth.

The equator is an imaginary line that runs around the middle of the Earth. It separates the Northern Hemisphere from the Southern Hemisphere. North America—where Canada, the United States, and Mexico are located—is in the Northern Hemisphere.

The Hemispheres

When the North Pole is tilted toward the sun, the sun's most powerful rays strike the northern half of the Earth and less sunshine hits the Southern Hemisphere. That is when people in the Northern Hemisphere enjoy summer. When

the North Pole is tilted away from the sun, and the Southern Hemisphere receives the most sunshine, the seasons reverse. Then winter comes to the Northern Hemisphere. Seasons in the Northern Hemisphere and the Southern Hemisphere are always opposite.

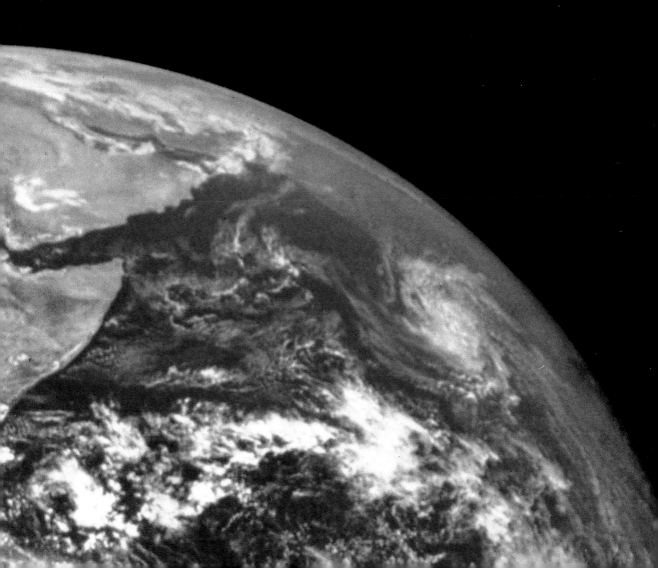

Get Ready for Kenya

Let's take a trip! Climb into your hot-air balloon and we'll drop in on a country on the east coast of Africa. Kenya is slightly smaller than the state of Texas and nearly 32 million people live here. Part of the country is bordered by the Indian Ocean. Kenya is famous for its beautiful scenery and for its wildlife, including elephants, lions, and giraffes.

The equator runs through Kenya. This means that the sun is directly overhead all year, so the climate is usually warm or hot.

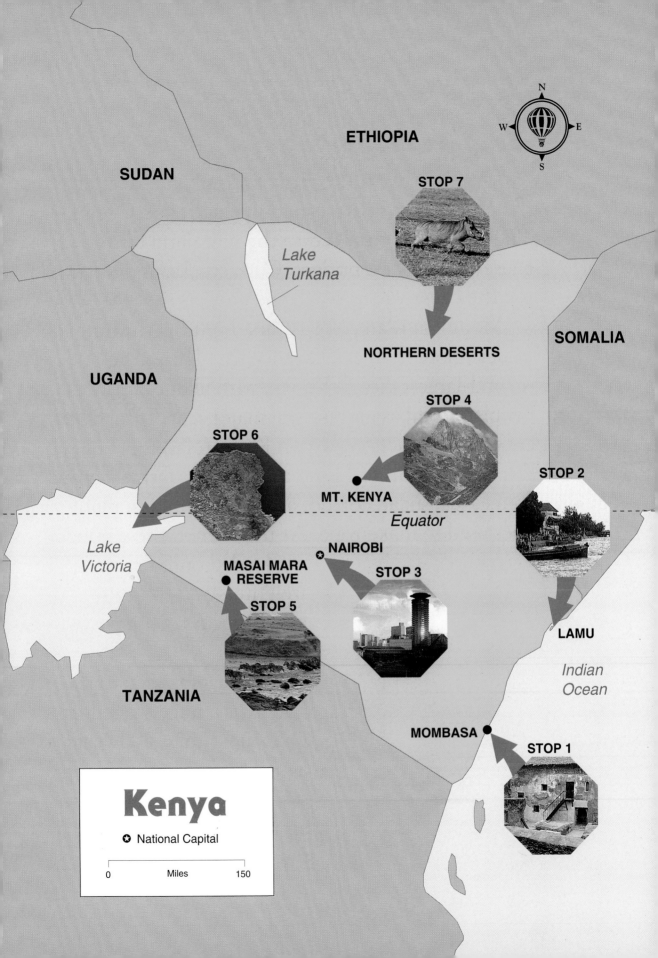

ETHIOPIA

SUDAN

STOP 7

Lake Turkana

SOMALIA

UGANDA

NORTHERN DESERTS

STOP 4

STOP 6

STOP 2

MT. KENYA

Equator

Lake Victoria

NAIROBI

MASAI MARA RESERVE

STOP 3

LAMU

STOP 5

Indian Ocean

TANZANIA

MOMBASA

STOP 1

Kenya

⊛ National Capital

0   Miles   150

Stop 1: Mombasa

Our first stop is the city of Mombasa. Most of the city is built on an island in the Indian Ocean. The island is connected to the mainland by a causeway and two bridges. Cars, trucks, and a railroad use the causeway to reach the city.

Mombasa is an old city, first built by Muslim traders more than 1,000 years ago. This is the second-largest city in Kenya, with about 600,000 people. Mombasa is also the major seaport for the country. Products grown on Kenyan farms are shipped by train to Mombasa. Kenya's farmers grow coffee, tea, sugar, cotton, and sisal. Sisal is a plant fiber used to make rope. At the harbor, these goods are loaded onto ocean freighters and then they are shipped to other countries.

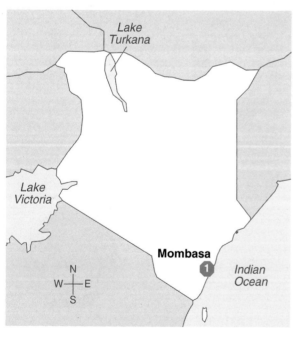

At the entrance to the harbor is a huge stone fort built more than 400 years ago. The fort is now a museum where you can learn about the many battles fought there.

In Mombasa, you can visit an old stone fort that is now a museum.

Most of Mombasa has changed little in the past 100 years. The newer office buildings and homes are on the outskirts or on the mainland. Modern hotels are strung along the coast of the mainland. Vacationers come from as far away as Europe to visit the Indian Ocean beaches near Mombasa.

*Next, we'll travel **northeast** to the island of Lamu.*

Dhows, or fishing boats, are always traveling in and out of Lamu's busy harbor.

Lake Turkana

Lake Victoria

Lamu

1

2

Indian Ocean

N
W E
S

SITAWA

Stop 2: Lamu

Lamu is also an island in the Indian Ocean, and the town of Lamu is the oldest in Kenya. Hundreds of years ago, Lamu was part of a society called Swahili. Swahili is a mixture of African and Muslim customs, ideas, and languages.

Lamu can only be reached by boat or plane. No cars or trucks are allowed on the island. People use donkey carts for transportation. There are very few modern buildings. The narrow, winding dirt streets are lined with walls and houses made of coral blocks, with roofs of tin or coconut palm leaves.

The harbor of Lamu is usually filled with fishing boats called *dhows*. These boats, each with a large sail, were used nearly 2,000 years ago.

The weather on Lamu is usually hot. You might want to stop at a drink house for a fruit shake, made with ice cream and mango, banana, or coconut.

*For our next stop, we'll head **northwest** to the city of Nairobi.*

A young boy uses his donkey cart to transport a bed.

Stop 3: Nairobi

Nairobi is the capital of Kenya and its largest city. A huge valley cuts through the center of Kenya from north to south. It is called the Great Rift Valley. Nairobi is located on highlands above the valley. It has warm days and cool nights.

The building of Nairobi began only 100 years ago. In the downtown area you will see mainly modern buildings.

Nairobi has one of the most unusual parks in the world—Nairobi National Park. From your car or bus, you can see wild animals roaming the grass-lands. There are zebras,

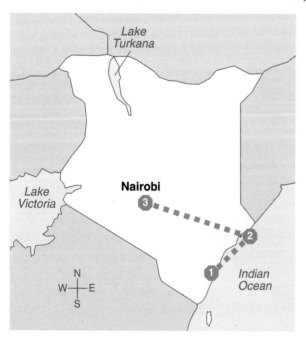

giraffes, lions, and dozens of other animals in the park. In a separate park, you can feed giraffes from a large wooden platform. Near the park entrance is a music and dance center called the Bomas of Kenya. Here you can see the traditional dances of 11 different tribal groups.

Above: A pride of lions rests in the tall grasses. Below: Tall, modern buildings make up the skyline of Nairobi.

Growing Up in Kenya

A little more than half the children in Kenya go to school. Lessons are taught in both Swahili and English. Children study geography, history, math, and science. They go to elementary school until age 11. Then about one out of every seven students goes on to secondary school.

In some village schools, children learn about farming and raising farm animals. Older people come to the school to teach tribal stories, dances, and crafts like wood carving and jewelry making.

The people of Kenya are divided into more than 40 different tribes. Some of the tribes live far from the cities and towns. The people of these tribes live by raising sheep, goats, cattle, and camels. Since they live too far away to attend schools, the children learn the skills they need from their parents.

Boys learn to herd the animals, and they also learn the traditional skills of warriors. Girls are taught to cook, tan leather, weave sisal rope into mats, and make repairs on the family's huts. Many girls also become expert basket weavers or jewelry makers. In many of these distant tribes, a few of the children are chosen to be sent away to school. When they return, these students have new skills and information that can help their tribe.

Schoolchildren from the Masai tribe gather together for a picture.

*Now we'll steer our hot-air balloon **northeast** to Mount Kenya.*

Clouds brush the top of Mount Kenya, the highest mountain in Kenya.

Stop 4: Mount Kenya

As our hot-air balloon leaves Nairobi, you can see Mount Kenya far in the distance. The mountain towers to a height of 17,058 feet. It is the highest mountain in Kenya.

Even though Mount Kenya is very close to the equator, the peaks are capped with snow and ice. The reason for this is that the air becomes cooler as you climb higher. Thousands of years ago, Mount Kenya was a volcano. Like most of the volcanoes in Kenya, it has not been active for many centuries.

In the foothills below the mountain, we pass tea and coffee plantations. Kenya is one of the world's important growers of tea and coffee. Farther up the mountain slopes, there are smaller farm villages. The Kikuyu and other tribes have farmed here for many years. In tribal religions, Mount Kenya is a sacred place. Still higher up the slopes, the land is covered by bamboo forests.

To the west, you can see Mount Elgon, Kenya's second-highest mountain. Mount Elgon was also once a volcano and has a huge crater almost 4 miles wide.

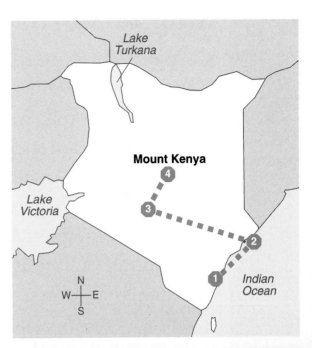

On a tea plantation, tea leaves are carefully picked by workers.

Next, *we'll travel* **southwest** *to Masai Mara Game Reserve.*

Stop 5: Masai Mara Game Reserve

We are now on the southwestern border of Kenya. The Masai Mara Game Reserve is one of about 40 national parks and game reserves in Kenya. These are special places for the protection of Africa's famous wild animals.

Masai Mara is part of an even larger reserve called the Serengeti Plain, which reaches south into the country of Tanzania. Each year, one of the most amazing migrations on Earth begins in June. About 2 million antelope, called wildebeests, suddenly start traveling north toward the fresher grass of Masai Mara. Soon, other animals join the march.

Thousands of zebras and wildebeests thunder across the Mara River during their yearly migration.

Lake Turkana

Lake Victoria

4

5   3

Masai Mara

2

1   Indian Ocean

N
W   E
S

Gazelles and 250,000 zebras gallop along. The animals' hoofbeats sound like thunder and the earth shakes.

Lions, leopards, and cheetahs follow along, ready to pounce on stray animals. Wild dogs and hyenas join the hunt, and vultures circle overhead.

From July to November, all of these animals roam through Masai Mara. There are also herds of elephants, giraffes, and buffalo, as well as hippos, crocodiles, storks, ostriches, and flamingos.

One day in November, the wildebeests will suddenly head south. The great Serengeti migration will begin again.

A cheetah guards her young cubs in the Masai Mara Game Reserve.

LET'S TAKE TIME OUT

The Foods of Kenya

For a Swahili breakfast in Kenya, you might try a porridge called *ugali*, or banana pancakes topped with honey.

A Kenyan tribal woman cooks fresh fish for her family over a small fire.

At lunchtime, Kenyans in the cities and towns can enjoy hamburgers or fish and chips (French fries). Dinner usually includes grilled meat or fish, or barbecued beef called *ngombe*. Another favorite is a meat stew made with coconut and coconut milk. With the main dish, you might have *maharagwe*, made with kidney beans, or *matoke*, made with corn and mashed plantains. Plantains are like bananas.

Many of the restaurants are owned by families who migrated to Kenya from India. Indian food is very different from Swahili. You might have an Indian dinner of *tandoori*, made with lamb, chicken, or fish. Many of the dishes are served with rice and a spicy flavoring of curry.

*For our next stop, we'll travel **northwest** to Lake Victoria.*

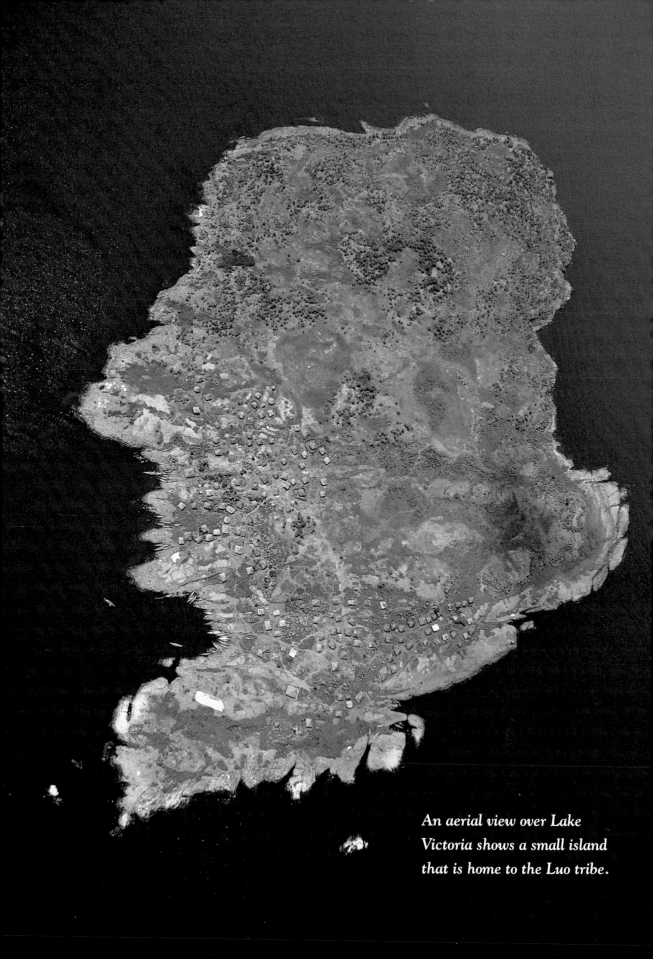

An aerial view over Lake Victoria shows a small island that is home to the Luo tribe.

Stop 6: Lake Victoria

As our hot-air balloon soars over western Kenya, we pass over green rolling hills. Below us, you can see farms and plantations growing cotton, sugarcane, tea, and sisal. Some of the houses are round, white-washed huts made of clay with thatch roofs. Other houses are square and have tin roofs.

Farther west, Lake Victoria shimmers in the bright sun. The lake is almost as large as the state of Maine. It is the third-largest lake in the world. Victoria is also the source of the Nile River, the longest river on Earth.

Lake Victoria is quite shallow. Farm and fishing villages dot the shore of the lake. Most of the people living here are members of the Luo tribe. Sailing in small *dhows*, Luo fishermen bring in large catches of fish every day. There are 200 kinds of fish in the lake, but most of the catch will be Nile perch.

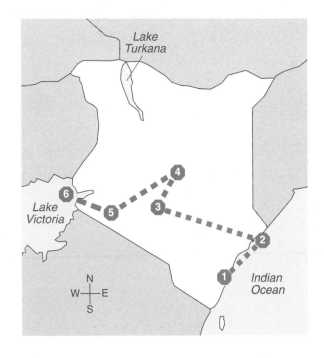

For our last stop, we'll head **northeast** into Kenya's northern deserts.

Stop 7: The Northern Deserts

Most of northern Kenya is desert or near-desert. Our hot-air balloon drifts over rugged mountains and the craters of ancient volcanoes that stopped erupting thousands of years ago. The air is hot and dry. In the hills around Lake Turkana, there is a thicker cover of trees and scrub. In this area, you might see elephants, antelopes, warthogs, baboons, and monkeys.

Warthogs are common in the near-deserts of northern Kenya.

A number of tribes live in this sun-baked, wild region. They raise sheep, goats, cattle, and usually some camels, which they use for milk. The tribespeople are nomads who move often in search of grass and water for their herds.

The northern tribes have lived this nomadic life for many generations. They know little about modern life in the cities and towns, but they prefer to live in the old way. Now and then, members of a tribe will visit a town to trade for cloth, tools, or other items. They are skilled in crafts, especially jewelry making. They make beautiful headbands, necklaces, and bracelets out of glass, beads, copper, and even plastic.

Hot-air balloons soar high above Kenya and make large shadows on the flat, dry land.

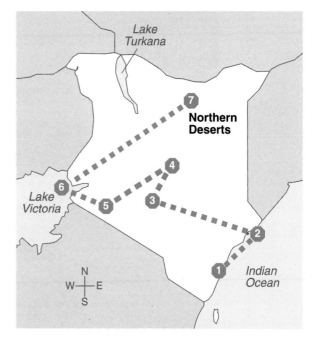

A Wildlife Safari

Safari is the Swahili word for "travel," and Kenya is the world's most popular country for wildlife safaris. Every year, more than 1 million people come here to travel on safari through the national parks and reserves.

Most safaris set out from Nairobi or Mombasa. With your safari guide, you travel in a group, riding in a minibus or Land Rover. The trip will last anywhere from 2 days to 2 weeks, or even longer. On

People on safari can photograph animals in natural settings. Here, a safari bus drives past a pair of giraffes.

some safaris, people stay at comfortable lodges inside the parks. Other travelers prefer to stay in tents and have meals cooked over an open fire.

Twice a day, your guide will take you on a "game drive" to see the animals. With your camera ready, you drive past herds of elephants, and you will probably see giraffes, zebras, baboons, and maybe a pride of lions. The other hunter animals, like leopards and cheetahs, are harder to spot. There will be many different kinds of antelope, such as Thomson's gazelle, wildebeests, impalas, and topi. You might even be lucky enough to spot a rhinoceros. At Masai Mara, you can even take a special safari by hot-air balloon.

In wooded areas you may come across different kinds of monkeys. There are snakes, too, including the cobra, puff adder, and python. At the end of the day, you can go for a swim in the lodge pool. Then, over a hearty dinner of grilled steaks or stew, everyone often talks about the exciting things they saw that day.

Now it's time to steer your hot-air balloon toward home. When you return, you can think back about your great adventure in Kenya.

Glossary

causeway A roadway built to connect an island with the mainland.

crater An opening at the mouth of a volcano.

dhow A small boat with a single sail, used on the Indian Ocean and Lake Victoria.

migration A move from one place to another; many animals and birds migrate with the seasons.

Muslims Followers of the religion of Islam.

nomads Members of a group or tribe who have no permanent home but move from place to place.

plantation A large farm with many workers where a single crop, such as coffee or tea, is grown and harvested.

pride A group of lions.

safari A trip into the parks and game reserves of east Africa.

scrub Low trees or shrubs.

source The place where a river begins.

summit The highest point of a mountain.

thatch A roof made of tree branches or palm leaves.

Further Reading

Bowden, Rob. *Changing Face of Kenya.*
    Raintree Steck Vaughn, 2002
Broberg, Catherine. *Kenya in Pictures.*
    Lerner Books, 2003
Daley, Patrick. *Kenya World Tour.* Steadwell, 2002
McNair, Sylvia. *Kenya (Enchantment of the World).*
    Children's Press, 2001
Saffer, *Barbara. Kenya.* Bridgestone Books, 2002

Suggested Web Sites

www.kenyaembassy.com/

www.kenya.go.ke

www.museums.or.ke/

www.kws.org/

www.geographia.com/kenya/

www.kenya.de/

Index

Acknowledgments and Photo Credits
Cover: ©Eric Horan/Gamma Liaison; pp. 4, 6–7: National Aeronautics and Space
Administration; p. 11: ©C. J. Collins/Photo Researchers, Inc.; p. 12: ©Herlinde Koelbl/Leo
de Wys, Inc.; pp. 13, 14–15, 26: Kenya Tourist Office; p. 17: ©Peter Skinner/Photo
Researchers, Inc.; p. 18: ©Peter Arnold, Inc.; p. 19: ©Richard Saunders/Leo de Wys, Inc.;
pp. 20–21: ©Gregory G. Dimijian, M. D./Photo Researchers, Inc.; p. 22: ©Sven-Olaf
Lindblad/Photo Researchers, Inc.; p. 23: ©Peggy/Yoram Kahana/Peter Arnold, Inc.; pp. 24,
27: ©Y. Arthus-Bertrand/Peter Arnold, Inc.; p. 28: ©W. Hille/Leo de Wys, Inc.
Maps by Blackbirch Graphics, Inc.

Dropping In On...

Pack your bags! You're going on a trip!

Open these pages and travel to a fascinating and far-away place. Fly above a country and touch down to explore its cities and natural beauty. Experience ancient cultures as you roam—you'll meet many wonderful people, including other kids, and you'll see how they live. Uncover the secrets of map-reading and navigation as you pilot a hot-air balloon across rainforests, deserts, and mountain tops. When your journey is complete, you'll return home with a better understanding of the world around you and happy memories of the new friends you met along the way.

Titles in the Series:
Canada
China
Egypt
India
Kenya
Mexico
Saudi Arabia
Spain

ISBN 1-58952-849-2